The Authe

The Authentic Gospel

JEFFREY E. WILSON

THE BANNER OF TRUTH TRUST

THE BANNER OF TRUTH TRUST
3 Murrayfield Road, Edinburgh EH12 6EL
P.O Box 621, Carlisle, Pennsylvania 17013, USA

*

© The Banner of Truth Trust 1990
First Published 1990
ISBN 0 85151 574 6

*

Typeset in 10½/11 Linotron Plantin at The Spartan Press Ltd.,
Lymington, Hants
and printed and bound in the U.K. by
Howie and Seath Ltd, Edinburgh.

Preface

This treatise was borne out of a deep conviction that modern-day Christianity, as it is in evidence in most places, is far removed from biblical roots. In fact, the deviation is so far from true Christianity, as it is revealed in the New Testament, that there is only a superficial resemblance.

I have written with specific objectives in mind:

1. To present the authentic gospel of Jesus Christ as it is revealed in the New Testament, and to expose the false gospel that has, for decades, been embraced and adopted by large numbers of professing Christians.

2. To straightforwardly expose some characteristics of the counterfeit Christianity this false gospel has produced, and to present the essence and characteristics of authentic Christianity.

For those who read this exposition, I have a very specific desire:

– That those who have been deceived and consoled by the false gospel and its accompanying false Christian experience may come to realize their false spiritual security.

– That those who are truly born of God may realize the urgency of understanding and presenting the authentic gospel and of living as Christ's followers in the midst of today's ungodly society.

A careful analysis of the present state of world-wide Christianity reveals an insidious development. Today's 'Christianity' is in a state of disarray and decay, and the condition is deteriorating year by year. The truth of God's Word has been watered down and compromised to reach a common denominator that will appeal to and accommodate the largest number of participants. The result is a hybrid Christianity which is essentially man-centred, materialistic and worldly, and shamefully dishonouring to the Lord Jesus Christ. This present degeneracy is due in large part to the erroneous gospel that is presented by many today around the world.

This gospel, which has prevailed for decades, is fundamentally contrary to the message that Jesus and his apostles presented. It has been called a 'cheap' or 'easy' gospel, resulting in what has been termed 'easy believism'. Tragically, it is the gospel that is being presented today in many evangelical and fundamentalist churches, by many foreign missionaries, by many radio and TV ministries and Christian organizations, at many Christian camps, and in much 'Christian' literature.

Basically, this gospel states that in order to be saved, a person must simply 'believe in', 'trust in', 'receive' or 'accept' Jesus as his 'personal Saviour', or believe that he died for his sins personally, or receive his 'free gift' of eternal life. This 'easy' gospel is devoid of any demand for repentance, whereby the individual must turn from his sins and deny himself as he comes to Christ for salvation. It is likewise devoid of any demand on the individual to commit himself to Jesus Christ as his Lord, with a sincere desire to follow and obey him completely. Many today are happy and even anxious to have Jesus as 'a Saviour', in order to have assurance of going to heaven. But few want him to reign over and control *every* part of their lives, on *his* terms. Therefore, this gospel which makes no such demands has

I

an ever-widening appeal and receives an ever-increasing 'positive' response.

Simply stated, this popular message calls people to receive Jesus as SAVIOUR so that they may go to heaven. But the only salvation in view is from the future penalty of sin. A separate appeal is then made *after* they have been 'saved'. This second appeal is to submit to Jesus as LORD, and to live in obedience to him. According to the proponents of this gospel, it is possible that a person who has become a Christian may never become Christ's disciple; that is, he may never choose to follow or obey him fully, or he may follow him for a time and stop. Nonetheless, based on the logic of this distorted gospel, such an individual will still be saved from the future punishment of hell if he has at some time sincerely received Jesus as 'personal Saviour'. He will, it is said, enter heaven but miss out on 'rewards'. In summary, one fundamental premise of this gospel is that commitment to the absolute rule of Jesus Christ in one's life is not necessary for salvation. Being his disciple is an 'option'.

In contrast to this, the authentic gospel of the New Testament entreats people to receive or submit to Jesus Christ as LORD and SAVIOUR. It does not appeal to us to be saved from sin with respect to its future penalty only. It simultaneously calls us to be saved now from sin and its consequences, to be freed from sin's bondage so as to follow Christ in obedience (*John* 8:31–36). The true gospel calls men to a life of discipleship and obedience to the principles and precepts presented in the New Testament. Certainly that is the call of Jesus' gospel, which contains the oft-repeated words, 'Follow me'. Jesus said, 'Not everyone who says to me, "Lord, Lord", will enter the kingdom of heaven; but he who does the will of my Father who is in heaven' (*Matthew* 7:21). Similarly, John wrote, 'The one who does the will of God abides forever' (*1 John* 2:17). Jesus' commission to his disciples was, 'Go and make *disciples*, . . . teaching them to obey all that I have commanded'. True Christians in any nation who have rightly believed in Christ *are* his disciples by nature of their initial commitment to him for salvation.

Discipleship is not a secondary option. There is abundant evidence in the New Testament to prove this.

The theological invention of men in which Jesus Christ as Saviour is distinguished from Jesus Christ as Lord is patently unbiblical. In his second letter, Peter referred to the 'Lord and Saviour Jesus Christ' (*2 Peter* 1:11; 2:20; 3:2; 3:18). He is ONE person of the Triune God. He is *not* divided. He is the ONE to whom a person entrusts himself for salvation from sin, now and forever. 'Believe on the Lord Jesus Christ and you will be saved', Paul told the Philippian jailer (*Acts* 16:31). To the Colossian believers he wrote, 'As you have received Christ Jesus the Lord . . .' (*Colossians* 2:6). Salvation is primarily a living *relationship* with the *Lord* and Saviour Jesus Christ.

Meaning of 'Believe'

It is not surprising that some may find this discussion confusing because faith or belief in Jesus Christ is the cornerstone of this false gospel as well as of the true gospel. Therefore, the critical question to be examined and resolved is this: What is the meaning of the word 'believe' and how is it explained or defined in the New Testament? Jesus was careful to define the essence of 'believe' as he used it with reference to himself. It is to believe that he is the Son of God, God in human flesh. It is to believe that he came to die in man's place, to pay the penalty for man's sin. It is to 'receive' him as the Messiah, the Saviour sent from God to rescue man from sin's penalty. This is where today's popular gospel stops. But this is only part of the gospel Jesus and his disciples presented.

Jesus' understanding of 'belief' in him contradicts today's prevailing gospel, which declares salvation to be a 'free gift' that costs a person *nothing*. Jesus unequivocally called men to 'calculate the cost' before making a decision to follow him.

According to his message, salvation costs a man *everything*. This additional sense of the concept of 'belief' is revealed in many passages in the Gospels, such as Matthew 16:24–27, Mark 1:14–15, Luke 14:25–33, Luke 18:18–30, and John 12:24–26. To believe in Jesus necessarily involves the *denial* of oneself, *forsaking* all one has and is in oneself and *repenting* or turning from one's self-centredness and sins to the Lord in unreserved *commitment*, with the conscious intention to *follow* and *obey* him. Therein lies the personal 'cost' that must be considered by anyone who would 'believe' in Christ for salvation. As in the first century, it seems that few people today want to pay that heavy price. It is still true, as Jesus taught, that 'the gate is small, and the way is narrow that leads to life, and few are those who find it'. That is, comparatively speaking, few there will be in any age or nation who will respond to the gospel that Jesus presented.

One specific example of Jesus' evangelistic message and method, of the many that could be cited from the Gospels, is the rich young ruler (*Luke* 18:18–25). This man was actually seeking the way to obtain eternal life. Though he professed to have kept God's commandments, Jesus knew his mind and motives. He was wealthy and apparently dependent upon his wealth. Did Jesus give this 'active seeker' an easy-formula gospel, with steps one, two, three? Clearly he did not. Jesus penetrated to the core of that to which the man was devoted and dependent upon when he called on him to repent, renouncing his self-centred attachment to his money and possessions. Jesus then said, '. . . and come, follow me'. Luke states that, after hearing Jesus' demands, 'the man became very sad; for he was extremely rich'. The man, though seemingly sincere in his desire for eternal life, did not have a true vision of life after this life, for his security rested in his earthly riches and possessions. He refused to submit to Jesus' condition, for the cost was too great. He loved what he had and he was not prepared to give it up. Jesus had taught on an earlier occasion that 'no one can serve two masters; for either he will hate the one and love the other, or he will hold to one and despise the other. You cannot serve God and riches' (*Matthew* 6:24). Jesus was simply proving to the

4

young ruler that he wanted eternal life on his own terms, not on God's terms. He wanted to do the impossible – love and serve two masters. Rather than try to encourage him to make a false decision, as many today would have done, Jesus let him leave and did nothing to persuade him. He knew the man was not truly convicted of his sins and therefore was not ready to repent and follow him unreservedly. The young man was not prepared to 'believe' in Christ, according to Jesus' definition.

There are millions in the western world who have made 'decisions' for Christ, who are, by comparison, as wealthy as that young ruler. However, if the same evangelistic message that Jesus gave to that man were being faithfully given to the affluent around the world, we fear that the response of many would be just that of the young ruler. They would be forced to count the cost, and all but a very few might turn away, unwilling to repent of their sins of greed, covetousness, idolatrous attachment to their money and possessions, and unwilling to change their primary devotion and dependence from earthly riches to God. As Jesus said, 'How hard it is for those who are wealthy to enter the kingdom of God. It is easier for a camel to go through the eye of a needle, than for a rich man to enter the kingdom of God.'

The sad fact is that many have weakened Jesus' message in order to appeal to those who are affluent. Most people in the West can be classified as affluent (relative to third-world standards) and many *are* responding to this gospel that presents no cost or sacrifice. They 'believe' in Christ with no serious intention of transferring their heart devotion to him. They basically retain their love of and attachment to their money and possessions, as well as the security and power it affords them. They are led to believe that Jesus received them and that they have eternal life. But he most assuredly does not receive them, any more than he did the young ruler. It would be infinitely better for them to be turned away by today's evangelists and churches, as Jesus turned people away, than to encourage them in their delusion.

Honest examination of the New Testament makes it clear that 'saving faith' is accompanied by *repentance* from sin and self. It is the unreserved commitment of one's life and eternal destiny to the Lord Jesus Christ. In fact, commitment is inherent in the meaning of faith. The Greek word for 'believe', *pisteuo*, can be translated into English as 'believe, commit, entrust, trust'. Thayer's Greek-English Lexicon gives one general definition of *pisteuo* as, 'to give oneself up to in faith'. With reference to belief in Christ in particular, it notes that 'obedience to Christ' is inherent in the definition. To believe is to enter into an intimate relationship with the Christ in whom faith is exercised and to acknowledge his authority with the result that his rule and character become manifest in the life of the believer. Those who thus believe will say at once with Saul of Tarsus, 'Lord, what will you have me to do?' (*Acts* 9:6).

The New Testament teaches that commitment of one's life to Jesus Christ is absolutely essential in true conversion. Simply stated, no person becomes a Christian who does not submit to Jesus Christ as his or her Lord, with a sincere intention to be his disciple and obey him fully. This is not to say that at the point of initial commitment a person understands all of the implications of discipleship or the rule of Christ in his life. Learning such implications is a lifelong process. Initially, he will only have the understanding of a child. But child-like faith, as all true faith, submits without any conscious reservations. This is a point yet to be amplified.

God's Condition: All or Nothing

The Bible is clear that salvation is God's work from beginning to end. Before anyone can repent and believe in Christ, there must be an inner work of the Spirit of God. The Spirit must produce conviction of sin and alter the individual's disposition from self and sin to God and righteousness. He convicts men of *sin*, of the *righteousness* of God (how sin is a violation of his righteous standards) and of

God's *judgment* of sin (*John* 16:8). He normally uses biblical preaching to produce such conviction (*1 Thessalonians* 1:5). When God has produced conviction of sin in us he calls us (*Romans* 8:30), and spiritually enlivens us to repent and believe (*2 Thessalonians* 2:13, 14), and thus we respond to the call of the gospel. 'All that the Father gives me shall come to me; and him that comes to me I will in no wise cast out' (*John* 6:37).

The Spirit of God convicts each person whom he is bringing to salvation. Some may be convicted of specific sins, others by the consciousness of their self-centred nature as well as specific sins. He produces a sense of the awfulness of sin in the light of God's holiness, and creates a sense of urgent need to be saved from self and from the consequences of sin. When we are convicted of our sins, we desire to turn from them and to renounce them forever. That is biblical *repentance*. We unreservedly cast ourselves upon Jesus Christ as our only hope for salvation from sin's bondage and consequences, with the sincere intent to obey him totally. That is biblical *commitment*. In the simplicity of our understanding at that point, we deny ourselves and our self-dependency and self-centredness. Forsaking all earthly security, we turn ourselves over entirely to Christ's control. We intend to follow and obey him, though we may not yet understand much of what it means, for we realize that he is the only One who can rescue us from our desperate state. To state it another way, it is impossible for us *not* to have the desire to obey the Lord's commandments. That would be to desire to continue in sin, which would mean we are not truly repentant. To carry the thought back another stage, it would indicate that we have not been truly convicted of sin and our wretched condition before God. Regardless of our apparent interest in being saved, we do not really want to be saved from sin if we want to continue sinning and disobeying the only One who can save us.

If a person has *any* reservations about obeying the Lord, or is unwilling to relinquish any thing or any sin, he is not ready to repent and believe in Christ for salvation. If such a person is encouraged to make a 'decision to be saved', there may be a response; but such a response, however sincere, is not true conversion.

In summary, commitment is always inherent in genuine faith, for it is the response of a person who has been personally convicted of sin by the Holy Spirit. Such conviction produces a sense of need for Jesus Christ and that need produces unreserved commitment to him. Wherever there is true faith there is spiritual conversion, which is seen in a *changed* life: 'If any man be in Christ, he is a new creation; the old things passed away; behold, new things have come' (*2 Corinthians* 5:17).

Results of Conversion

The most wonderful result of true conversion is spiritual union with Jesus Christ. Fellowship with Christ and communion with God grow from this union (*1 John 1:3*). Fellowship with Christ stimulates love for him which in turn produces devotion and obedience to him (*John* 14:15, 20, 21; 15:4, 5). But this devotion and obedience are not complete immediately. As was mentioned earlier, when a person first comes to know Christ, though he is sincere in his desire and intention to obey him, he probably does not understand much of the day-to-day implications of all that his new relationship means. But he is born of God, he has a new life, and there will be an on-going process of new obedience. As the Spirit works in his life there will be, to one degree or another, *continuing* commitment to the rule of Christ and submission to his Word (see *Romans* 8:2–16). The Christian life is one of progressive spiritual growth. If there has been spiritual birth, there is spiritual life; and if there is life, there will be growth – slow at times, faster at others, but continuing as believers are prepared for heaven. But if there is no growth, there is no life. The New Testament calls this growth process 'sanctification'. It begins at conversion.

Sanctification is a sovereign act of God in which he separates his people to himself. By definition, it is 'to be made holy'. Biblical sanctification includes three aspects: past, present, and future. One who is born of God and converted *has been* (*1 Corinthians* 6:11) and is *presently* being sanctified, or made holy (*Romans* 6:22; *Ephesians* 5:26). In the future, he *will be* fully set apart to the Lord, sin having been removed totally (*Romans* 8:23, 30; *Ephesians* 5:27). Both the past and the present aspects of sanctification are essential if we are to have a legitimate hope of being set apart to the Lord forever. Hebrews 12:14 is referring to the present aspect of sanctification when it states, 'Pursue the sanctification without which no one will see the Lord.'

Jesus prayed for the present sanctification of his disciples, 'Sanctify them in the truth; Thy word is truth' (*John* 17:17). His petition was that true believers might grow in practical holiness through their understanding of and obedience to the Word of God. Likewise, Paul prayed for the Colossian Christians, 'We have not ceased to pray for you and to ask that you may be filled with the knowledge of his will (as presented in his Word) . . . so that you may walk (live) in a manner worthy of the Lord, to please him in all respects, bearing fruit in every good work and increasing in the knowledge of God'. His prayer was that they would be holy, devoted to the Lord, in each detail of daily life, so as to please him.

The Scriptures give many examples of the practical holiness which develops in the experience of a Christian. They include: love for and devotion to God's Word; love for fellow Christians and for all men; control of fleshly desires; nonconformity to the world's mind-set and ways (since our minds are renewed by the gospel); modesty of lifestyle, of dress, and of physical appearance; and eternal investment through sacrificial living and giving.

Of course, we may suffer lapses in the process of growing in our knowledge of God and devotion to Christ. But the Spirit of Christ is always at work in the Christian to produce the necessary conviction, to discipline if necessary, and then to lead him to put to death the deeds of the flesh and to abide in Christ and live by the Spirit, bearing his fruit (*Hebrews* 12:7–11; *Romans* 8:9–14; *Galatians* 5:16–23; *John* 14:26 and 15:4,5).

The ministry of the Holy Spirit within us does not negate our responsibility; we must respond to his conviction and discipline. We must put off the 'old', be renewed in our minds by means of God's Word, and put on the 'new' (*Romans* 8:12; *Romans* 12:2; *Ephesians* 4:22–24). The apostle Paul knew that God is working in a Christian's life from start to finish (*Philippians* 1:6), yet all of his letters deal at some point with the Christian's responsibility to 'do'. His logic is, 'Work out your salvation . . . for God is at work in you, both to will and to do of his good pleasure' (*Philippians* 2:12,13). These are parallel truths that meet only in the mind of God.

From the above discussion, we see that the New Testament condemns the teaching which is popular today which states that a truly saved person does not *necessarily* show evidence of having been converted; or that he may not show significant change in his life; or that there may not be spiritual growth, though he has spiritual life; or that he may continue sinning wilfully and yet be saved in the end.

Assurance and Evidence

In contrast to this teaching, we must affirm that anyone who truly repents and commits himself to the Lord Jesus Christ does experience a definite and recognizable change of mind and inclination; inevitably there is genuine *evidence* of that change. He continues to trust in Jesus Christ alone for his salvation. He has a love for the Lord and a love for his Word. His desire is to live for the Lord and not for himself. Hence, his daily intention and pursuit is to learn and obey his commandments in all details of life, whatever the personal cost or apparent sacrifice. He progressively manifests the fruit of the Spirit as presented in Galatians 5:22–23. And he hates everything he recognizes as sin and wants to be free of it.

When a true Christian does sin or disobey God's Word in some particular, he feels conviction and guilt, and desires to turn from it. This is further evidence of the sanctifying work of the Holy Spirit. Romans 8:14–15 refers to this ministry of the Spirit within God's people: 'All who are being led by the Spirit of God – (led to put to death the deeds of the body, v.13) – *these* are sons of God'. No Christian can ever 'get away with' sinning. The indwelling Spirit of Christ produces conviction and aversion to sin (note *Galatians* 5:17). This conviction is part of his inner 'witness' to us that we are the children of God (*Romans* 8:16). Once the Spirit brings awareness and conviction of sin, there always follows a turning away from sin in practical repentance. In this world, to be sure, there will always be struggle and conflict with indwelling sin, but there cannot be continuing *practice* of any sin by one who is born of God. On the contrary, right-eousness is the goal and practice of his daily life (*1 John* 2:29; 3:9).

A further indication of genuine conversion and our new relationship to God as our Father is his *discipline* and correction (*Hebrews* 12:4–11), and the obedience which it produces. 'But if you are without discipline, of which all have become partakers, then you are illegitimate children and not sons'.

Such evidence as I am referring to here is a principal basis of biblical assurance of salvation. I say 'a principal' because evidence in the life is not the *only* basis for assurance. The Christian trusts in Christ's work *for* him before he knows the Spirit's work *in* him, and direct faith in Christ remains the primary form of assurance. But the Scriptures make clear that where faith is genuine it will always be accompanied by other evidence. The security of the Christian's relationship with God rests in God's grace alone, grace which led to the substitutionary sacrifice of Christ for man's sin and his present intercession (*Hebrews* 7:25). But a professing Christ-ian's *assurance* that he has a secure relationship with God through Christ has to be related to his continuance in faith and to the daily evidence of conversion and sanctification. Many passages in the New Testament teach that *present* evidence, not a past 'decision' or 'experience', is essential to a Christian's personal assurance (in addition to those already noted, the following texts are noteworthy: *II Corinthians* 13:5; *I John* 2:3–6; 15–17, 29; 3:7–9, 11, 14, 15; *James* 2:14–26; *Galatians* 5:19–24; 6:7, 8; *2 Peter* 1:4–11; *Hebrews* 10:36).

Commitment – Climax and Process

The commitment to Jesus Christ which leads to final salvation is two-fold: an initial decision and a continuing process.

When a person repents and entrusts himself to Jesus Christ as his Saviour from sin and the Lord of his life, it is, in a sense, a radical commitment. Before this point of decision, he has been accustomed to living his life under his own control and doing as he pleases. A critical turning point occurs when he finally decides to deny himself and forsake his self-pleasing so that Christ alone may henceforth control his life.

On the basis of this initial consecration the process of commitment begins. The Christian's ongoing desire and prayer is 'that I may know Christ' (*Philippians* 3:10) and be changed into greater conformity to him in heart and life. Thus by the constant aid of the Holy Spirit, the process of 'present' sanctification and discipleship continues to the end of our earthly sojourn.

One passage in which this process of commitment is described is Romans 12:1–2. On the basis of the love and grace of God which Paul had expounded in chapters 1 to 11, he exhorts the Christians in Rome to commit themselves to the Lord's rule and control. The motivation for such commitment is love for the Lord and appreciation for all he has done for them in providing their salvation (cf. *II Corin-*

thians 5:14–15). He indicates in verse 2 that this commitment will be manifested in a transformed life, conformed to the 'will of God' in everything. Paul's statement about not being 'conformed to the world' implies that the ways of God are in total contrast to the ways of the world, which is under Satan's control. He also indicates that it is by the 'renewing' of the mind that one is transformed and is enabled to 'prove' the will of God in specific areas of life. The mind of a Christian is renewed by means of God's Word. By its teaching the Christian is increasingly enlightened by the Holy Spirit concerning the specific areas of his life in which he must 'deny ungodliness and worldly desires' (*Titus* 2:12) and commit himself to the Lord's governing control. Because a Christian's mind is never finally fully 'renewed' in the practical experience and implementation of God's Word, commitment to the Lord cannot be a single once-for-all act or decision. Growth in understanding of God's will and an accompanying commitment and obedience to the Lord is, therefore, a continuing process in the life of every Christian, as is seen in Romans 12:1–2.

Unfortunately this passage is sometimes mistakenly used by those who try to differentiate between acceptance of Jesus as Saviour and commitment to Jesus as Lord. They base their interpretation of these verses on the presupposition that commitment of one's life to Christ is possible only after conversion, otherwise it would be a 'work'. They say that Paul gives doctrinal explanation of the 'gospel' in the earlier chapters of the letter. Beginning then with chapter 12, he presents instruction for those who have already responded positively to this gospel. As their argument goes, Romans 12:1 contains the first mention of commitment of one's life to Christ. Therefore, it obviously is not part of the faith (described earlier in the letter) that produces eternal salvation. Paul, they say, is urging those who have been saved through faith (without commitment) now to commit themselves to Christ. From this interpretation of verse 1, the logical implication in the urgent tone of Paul's plea is that these 'saved' people may or may not commit themselves to Christ's rule.

The foregoing argument overlooks a key passage in Romans 6:13–22. This passage clearly refers to two kinds of commitment: that which results in eternal life (i.e. salvation) in contrast to that which results in death. In Romans 6, Paul is further defining the faith that produces salvation, which he introduced and expounded in chapters 3 to 5. Romans 6:16 and 22 are examples; 'Do you not know that when you present yourselves to someone as slaves for obedience, you are slaves of the one whom you obey, either of sin resulting in death, or of obedience resulting in righteousness? . . . But now, having been freed from sin and enslaved to God (through union with Christ in regeneration), you derive your benefit, resulting in sanctification (practical holiness and growth), and the outcome, eternal life'. As we noticed earlier, Romans 8:2–16 also indicates commitment to the Lord as essential for and inherent in a true experience of salvation.

The Roman Christians to whom Paul wrote had already committed themselves to the Lord, having responded to the gospel in the 'obedience of faith' (1:5). And they were certainly continuing the process of commitment, for their faith was being proclaimed throughout the whole world (1:8), and the report of their obedience had become known to all (16:19). In Romans 15:14, 15, Paul says, 'My brethren, I myself also am convinced that you yourselves are full of goodness, filled with all knowledge, and able to admonish one another, but I have written very boldly to you on some points, so as to remind you again.' The Christians in Rome were obviously committed to the Lord and were obeying him. However, although they were doing so well, he knew they needed 'reminders'. That is why he gives so much exhortation to them throughout the letter, including the words of Romans 12:1–2.

14

Summing up the Heresy

Too many professedly evangelical churches and ministries today are presenting and promoting an adulterated gospel. The advocates of this gospel believe that a person is saved by 'simple faith' (according to *their* definition of faith). He is on his way to heaven, ticket secured. He is 'justified', but may yet have to experience practical 'sanctification'. After presumed conversion, in order that he may be sanctified, the person is urged to submit to the Lordship of Christ, become his disciple, follow and obey him and present his body a living sacrifice. But he may choose not to; the choice is his. In other words (to state it more bluntly), there are Christians who commit their lives to Christ, live for him and obey him; but there are also Christians who do not fully submit to Christ, will not live for him, and will continue to disobey him, living in sin and rebellion. These are classified as 'carnal Christians' or 'backslidden Christians'. Those who follow and obey Christ will receive 'rewards' in heaven. Those who choose to stay 'carnal' and not follow or obey him in everything will not receive rewards. But they still have the assurance of heaven, because they 'believed in' or 'accepted Jesus' as their personal Saviour at some time in their lives.

Untold millions around the world who have made 'simple-faith decisions' have lived or are living in blatant disobedience to God's Word. Consequently a 'doctrinal' explanation or rationale for such clear contradiction had to be invented. That is why this theological argument has evolved. It is an indisputable distortion of the gospel of Christ and it is to be classified as unqualified heresy. Satan is manifestly using it to undermine biblical and historic Christianity world-wide.

Consequences of the Heresy

Even in the midst of this distortion of New Testament truth, God in his mercy sometimes brings sinners to himself. But it is also evident that the teaching I have described produces many 'decisions' which are not Spirit-wrought conversions. Sadly, there are professing Christians who have been taught that they are born again and eternally secure, when their lives clearly belie their profession. They have been left with a false assurance that they are going to heaven when in fact they are not. This is a tragic consequence of the heresy. To have a part in such gross deception is reprehensible. Anyone who in ignorance presents or encourages this false gospel will be held accountable to the Lord and justly judged by him, according to 1 Corinthians 3:10–15. It is to be feared that those who consciously and resolutely persist in presenting this heresy are products of it themselves and are false teachers, regardless of their profession or 'Christian' reputation. They are doomed to a tragic destiny according to Paul's sobering declaration in Galatians 1:8–12.

True Christians have an obligation to be aware of the false gospel and to avoid its erroneous terminology and simplistic appeals. There is little doubt that if more evangelists and would-be evangelists were delivering a truly biblical message, far fewer 'decisions for Christ' would be made, thus averting some of the growing consequences of the heresy. Additionally, some so-called 'carnal Christians' would possibly come to realize their false security and come to Christ in true humility, repentance and genuine faith.

It is imperative that all who have been born of God be careful to present a biblically-accurate gospel message. Care must be taken not to encourage a premature decision, which is sometimes a temptation, especially when the evangelist has a sincere concern for people's spiritual welfare. There must be contentment in patiently waiting on the Lord to use the biblical message to produce a 'new creation' in Christ. For only he can do so.

Above and beyond the tragic consequence of false decisions and false assurance resulting from the deception of the modern gospel, there is a more serious consequence. It is an affront to the Sovereign Lord to assure a self-centred sinner that he can be saved eternally through 'simple' faith in Christ and then to encourage that 'saved' sinner that he is securely saved even although he wilfully continues disobeying the One who is supposed to have saved him. This faulty theological logic is nothing less than sheer mockery of the sacrifice of Christ and the grace and holiness of God. Hebrews 10:26–29 unambiguously states the dreadful consequence for those who have so 'insulted the Spirit of grace'.

Paul's letter to the Galatians presents a timely warning: 'Do not be deceived, God is not mocked; for whatever a man sows, this he will also reap. For the one who sows to his own flesh shall from the flesh reap corruption, but the one who sows to the Spirit shall from the Spirit reap eternal life' (*Galatians* 6:7–8).

Matthew Henry incisively comments on these verses: 'Those who go about to mock God do but deceive themselves. Spiritual hypocrisy is the greatest wickedness as well as folly, since the God with whom we have to do can easily see through all disguises, and will certainly deal with men hereafter, not according to their professions, but according to their practices.' Indeed, the proof of the profession is in the life's practices: thoughts, words, and conduct.

The final and most far-reaching consequence of the heresy is the degenerate form of Christianity it is producing. Yet so widespread, so commonplace has it become that it is by and large regarded as 'normal' Christianity.

The New Religion

What are we to make of the hybrid Christianity that this substandard and sadly incomplete and heretical gospel has produced? Is it Christianity? Or what is it?

Basically, what has evolved through the widespread propagation of today's popular gospel is a strange religion. It could be classified as the 'Christian' religion, for it is professedly founded upon Jesus Christ. It is likewise founded on orthodox beliefs (at least on the surface), such as the deity of Christ, the virgin birth of Christ, the infallibility of the Bible, Christ's resurrection and second coming, heaven and hell, a gospel based upon 'faith' rather than 'works', the new birth, and so forth. Because of this apparently sound foundation, this 'religion' is all the more subtly disguised and difficult to discern. It claims to be based upon the Bible exclusively. However, it is the Bible drastically watered down and distorted by accommodation and worldly-mindedness. Therefore much of the *teaching* of this religion, though ostensibly drawn from the Bible, is largely of man's invention and interpretation. This has clearly given an entirely new meaning and appearance to Christianity.

This Christian religious movement has no shortage of preachers, teachers, evangelists, missionaries, and writers. Seminaries, Bible schools and ministries of every sort turn them out by the myriads each year. The body of literature is likewise abundant, and growing monthly. As a result of such numerous and extensive channels of propagation this religion is multiplying its numbers and its influence at a phenomenal rate world-wide. Because it is the only 'Christianity' that many see and know today, to suggest that much of it is not fully biblical is to be branded as a fanatic, as a cynic, even as a heretic. Yet, the whole burden of the New Testament and legitimate Church history cries out in judgment against this worldly, man-centred manipulation of Christianity.

What does it all mean in practical terms? It means that there are many professing Christians in evangelical and fundamentalist churches, as well as in liberal churches, who have simply become participants in a religion, just as have the Mormons or Jehovah's Witnesses or Muslims, or members of any other religious movements. Presumably, these 'Christians' have each made some 'decision' in response to a gospel appeal, and have 'believed' in Christ in some manner. They quickly learn the language and ways of this religion as it is represented in their local church environment. In fact, many learn the 'truths' of this religion quite well, and can converse and write at length on 'spiritual' matters. Many are quite sincere and fervent in their religious experience. Many do a lot of 'religious' things; they are 'actively involved'. Some have a high level of zeal, actively promoting the 'gospel'. Many find great comfort, enjoyment and satisfaction in the fellowship of those in their local church, and a deep social need is met. Emotions are sometimes very much a part of this religious experience, individually and corporately. The characteristics noted here are certainly not unique to the Christian religion. Some are generic characteristics to be observed in many religions or religious movements around the world.

Most of these religious evangelicals undoubtedly believe they are 'born again' Christians, due to the false definitions that have evolved over the past years. That is to say, they believe they are born again, because they have been taught so. Thus, a 1985 Gallup poll revealed a most incredible statistic: approximately 40% of the adult population in the USA claim to be 'born again Christians'. What the poll does not reveal is that the real biblical meaning of the term 'born again' has been all but lost.

Some may wish to point out that if people are genuinely sincere in the decision they make concerning Christ, even if it is in response to a faulty gospel, God will honour their sincerity and save them. However, nearly every religion in the world is peopled with those who have made a genuinely sincere decision to embrace the teaching of their religion. Sincerity cannot save us.

In the light of the subtlety of Satan's masterful scheme of deception and the havoc it has created, it might seem nearly impossible for a person to know whether he or she is truly born of God or merely a participant in the 'born-again' religion. It is true that we cannot know with full certainty the spiritual condition of others, although Jesus does underline that those who are truly born again will be identifiable by the kind of spiritual fruit they produce. We *can* know about ourselves, for by the witness and light of the Holy Spirit we may know whether he is at work within our hearts. Is there an exclusive reliance upon Jesus Christ to save us from destruction? Is there an awareness of fellowship with Christ? Is there a heart for self-denial and sincere love for the Lord and a yearning to please him always? Is there a detachment from reliance on earthly possessions and securities? Is there practical avoidance of indulgence in pleasures which God's Word disallows? Is there a concern to redeem the time? Is there evidence of practical holiness? Is there distinctive love for other true Christians? Is there definite inner conviction and guilt whenever we knowingly violate any commandment or principle set forth in the New Testament? Is there a hatred of sin and a desire to abstain from all wickedness, even to abstain from every form or manifestation of evil (including, for example, that found in many television programmes)? If the answer to these questions is in the affirmative, then we can know we are born of *God* (*1 John* 2:29; 3:9; 4:7; 5:1–4) and not simply part of the 'Christian religion'.

Conclusion

With the unprecedented confusion that exists today concerning Christianity, there *must* be a strong clarification of these issues. God told Jeremiah that before he could build and plant he had to pluck up, break down and destroy (*Jeremiah* 1:10). Such must be done with this false gospel of cheap, easy believism, and the consequences of shameful 'Christian' living it produces. There is an urgent need for the true gospel and the radical truth of God's Word to be carefully defined and spread abroad wherever the infection has spread. May it be so, as God wills, for his glory and the preservation of authentic Christianity.

SOME OTHER BANNER OF TRUTH TITLES

TODAY'S GOSPEL –
Authentic or Synthetic?
Walter Chantry

In this arousing work Walter Chantry expounds from Christ's dealing with the Rich Young Ruler the essential elements in Gospel preaching. A close examination of the Scripture evidence leads to this conclusion:

'Differences between much of today's preaching and that of Jesus are not petty; they are enormous. The chief errors are not in emphasis or approach but in the heart of the Gospel message. Were there a deficiency in one of the areas mentioned in these pages, it would be serious. But to ignore all – the attributes of God, the holy law of God, repentance, a call to bow to the enthroned Christ – and to pervert the doctrine of assurance, is the most vital mistake.

'Incredulity may grip you. Can so many evangelicals be so wrong? . . . All are not in error, but great hosts are. All have not perverted the gospel to the same degree, but many are terribly far from the truth. All those who "make decisions" are not deceived, but great numbers are. Above all, few *care* to recover the Gospel message . . .'.

This powerfully-written book has a message which goes to the heart of the contemporary problem in a way that conferences and commissions on evangelism have failed to do. Its expository approach is particularly valuable.

Walter Chantry was born in 1938 at Norristown, Pennsylvania, raised in the Presbyterian Church; graduated B.A. in History from Dickinson College, Carlisle in 1960, and B.D. from Westminster Theological Seminary in 1963, from which time he has been pastor of Grace Baptist Church, Carlisle.

ISBN 0 85151 027 2

96pp., Paperback

GOD CENTRED EVANGELISM
R. B. Kuiper

'Here', writes John Murray, 'we have the theology of evangelism, and evangelism without scriptural theology has lost its moorings. R. B. Kuiper's writing, as his preaching and lecturing, was always characterized by clarity and simplicity'.

The book begins with God as the author of evangelism, and shows the relation of his love, election, covenant and commission to it. There are chapters on the scope, urgency, motive, aim, agent, approach, means, message, method, effectiveness and triumph of evangelism. Dr Kuiper also deals with zeal for, co-operation in, and resistance to evangelism.

A student of B. B. Warfield, on whom he made a deep impression, Dr Kuiper had a distinguished career in the pastoral and teaching ministry. He was President of Calvin College (1930–33) and Professor of Practical Theology at Westminster Theological Seminary (1933–52).

ISBN 0 85151 110 4

248pp., Paperback